REUSABLE STICKERS
Ruth's Story
Adapted from the book of Ruth

Retold by Laura Kelly
Illustrated by Nancy Pistone

Naomi was very sad. Her husband and two sons had died. Naomi decided to go to Bethlehem where she had some relatives.

So Naomi set off, and her daughters-in-law, Ruth and Orpah, went with her.

"You should go back to your parents," Naomi told her daughters-in-law. Orpah kissed Naomi goodbye, but Ruth clung to Naomi.

"Do not ask me to leave you," Ruth said. "Every place you live I will live. Your people will be my people. Your God will be my God."

Ruth and Naomi reached Bethlehem during the harvest. Ruth began to visit a local farmer's field to search for leftover grain.

Boaz, the owner of the field, asked a worker who Ruth was. "She wanted to follow behind us and gather the leftover grain," he told him.

Boaz told his farm workers to leave extra grain for Ruth to gather.

By the end of the day, Ruth had a lot of grain to take home to Naomi. Ruth told Naomi how kind Boaz had been.

Ruth gathered grain in Boaz' field every day until the harvest was over.

Before long, Boaz fell in love with Ruth. One day, Boaz asked Ruth to marry him.

Ruth and Boaz had a baby boy. They named him Obed.

Naomi was now very happy. God had looked after her. She thanked God for Ruth, Boaz, and Obed.

Ruth

Naomi

Orpah

field worker

field workers

Boaz

Naomi

Obed